TOOLS OF WAR

WEAPONS and VEHICLES of the IRAQ WAR

by Elizabeth Summers

Reading Consultant:
Barbara J. Fox
Professor Emerita
North Carolina State University

Blazers Books are published by Capstone Press,
1710 Roe Crest Drive, North Mankato, Minnesota 56003.
www.capstonepub.com

Library of Congress Cataloging-in-Publication Data
Summers, Elizabeth.
  Weapons and vehicles of the Iraq War / by Elizabeth Summers.
    pages cm.—(Blazers books. Tools of war)
  Includes bibliographical references and index.
  Summary: "Describes various weapons and vehicles used by U.S. and Iraqi forces during the
Iraq War"—Provided by publisher.
  Audience: Grades K-3.
  ISBN 978-1-4914-4081-0 (library binding)
  ISBN 978-1-4914-4115-2 (ebook pdf)
1. Iraq War, 2003-2011—Equipment and supplies—Juvenile literature. 2. Vehicles, Military—
History—21st century—Juvenile literature. 3. Iraq War, 2003-2011—Transportation—Juvenile
literature. I. Title.
  DS79.763.S86 2016
  956.7044'3—dc23   2015006132

Editorial Credits

Anna Butzer, editor; Heidi Thompson, designer; Jo Miller, media researcher;
Katy LaVigne, production specialist

Photo Credits

BigStockPhoto.com: Johanson09, 15; DoD photo by Senior Master Sgt. Meneguin, U.S. Air Force,
cover; Dreamstime: Robert Sholl, 5; iStockphoto: Rockfinder, 29, Steevvoh, 22-23; Shutterstock:
Camptoloma, 24, Denis Kornilov, 11 (bottom), Militarist, 11 (top), zimand, 9 (bottom); U.S. Air
Force photo by Senior Airman Christina D. Ponte, 20-21, Staff Sgt. Aaron D. Allmon II, 18-19, Tech.
Sgt. Sabrina Johnson, 26-27; U.S. Army photo by Spc. Aaron L. Rosencrans, 17; U.S. Marine Corps
photo by Cpl. Kenneth Jasik, 13; Wikimedia: Photo Courtesy of PEO Soldier, 9 (top),
US Air Force, 6-7

Design Elements:
Shutterstock: angelinast, aodaodaodaod, artjazz, Brocreative, ilolab, kasha_malasha, Peter Sobolev

Printed in the United States of America in North Mankato, Minnesota.
052015   008823CGF15

TABLE OF CONTENTS

BOMBING OF BAGHDAD

The Iraq War (2003–2011) started when the United States and its **allies** bombed Baghdad, the capital of Iraq. Saddam Hussein was the leader of Iraq. Many experts believed that Iraq was building **weapons of mass destruction** (WMDs).

ally–a person or country that helps and supports another
weapon of mass destruction–nuclear, radiological, biological, chemical, or another weapon that can kill or harm a large number of people

Fact

The term "weapon of mass destruction" was first used in 1937. It described a German air force attack on a town in Spain.

armored humvee

The United States and its allies crushed Hussein's forces. But **insurgents** fought against the new Iraqi government. The war lasted for eight years as the United States and its allies fought against the insurgents. Many different weapons and vehicles were used.

insurgent—a person who rebels and fights against his or her country's ruling government and those supporting it

WEAPONS

Rifles and Machine Guns

Both U.S. troops and insurgents used lightweight weapons in close **combat**. These included rifles and machine guns. They had to be carefully cleaned to prevent damage caused by sand.

	M4 Assault Rifle	M24 Sniper Rifle	Soviet AKM rifle
Rate of Fire	700–950 rounds per minute	20 rounds per minute	600 rounds per minute
Weight	6.3 pounds (2.9 kg)	11.8 pounds (5.4 kg)	6.8 pounds (3.1 kg)
Firing Range	up to 656 yards (600 m)	up to 1,640 yards (1,500 m)	up to 1,094 yards (1,000 m)

combat–fighting between people or armies
range–the longest distance at which a weapon can still hit its target

M4 assault rifle

Fact
The Soviet AKM rifle is thought to be one of the best firearms ever made.

Soviet AKM rifle

The M249 Squad Automatic Weapon is the perfect mix of a machine gun and a rifle. It fires many rounds very quickly, like a machine gun. It also hits targets accurately and is easy to carry, like a rifle.

	M249 Squad Automatic Weapon	PKM Machine Gun
Rate of Fire	800 rounds per minute	650–750 rounds per minute
Weight	17 pounds (8 kg)	17 pounds (8 kg)
Firing Range	up to 3,940 yards (3,603 m)	up to 1,640 yards (1,500 m)

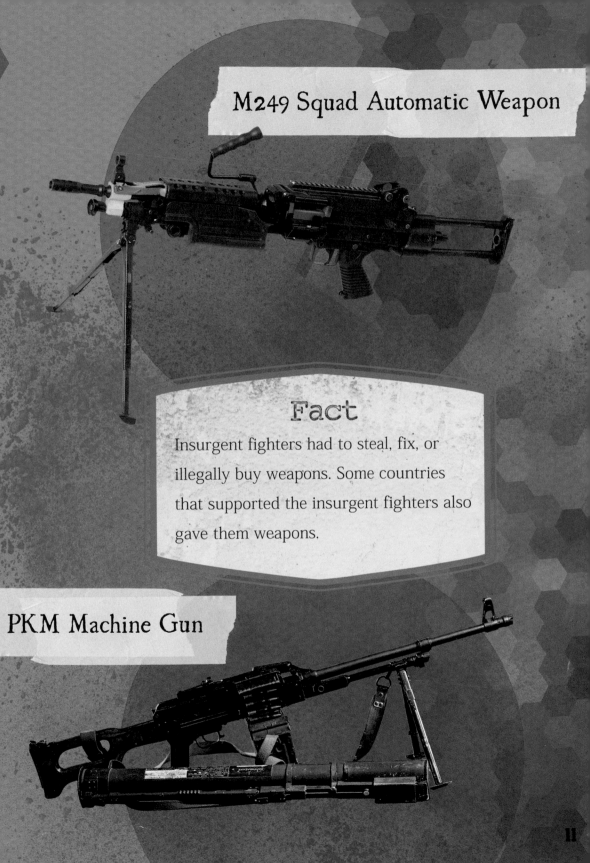

M249 Squad Automatic Weapon

Fact

Insurgent fighters had to steal, fix, or illegally buy weapons. Some countries that supported the insurgent fighters also gave them weapons.

PKM Machine Gun

Explosives

Explosives are an important part of modern **warfare**. During the Iraq War, the U.S. forces and their allies used weapons that launched explosives. The M32 multiple-shot grenade launcher could shoot six grenades in under three seconds.

Fact

The M32 multiple-shot grenade launcher weighs 11.7 pounds (5.3 kg). It can launch a grenade to a distance of about 437 yards (400 m).

warfare–the fighting of wars

M32 grenade launcher

Insurgents often used improvised explosive devices (IEDs). They were made with pieces from different weapons. Insurgents threw IEDs or buried them in roads to explode vehicles.

Fact

Remote controls or cell phones could be used to make IEDs explode.

improvised explosive device

Large Guns, Missiles, and Missile Defense Systems

Large guns and missiles destroyed enemy targets. Some were fired from military bases. Other missiles were moved to battle sites. Helicopters delivered M777 **howitzers** to battefields. Howitzers could fire rounds at targets up to 19 miles (31 km) away.

Fact

U.S. Tomahawk **cruise missiles** could be launched from ships or submarines. These missiles could hit targets up to 1,550 miles (2,494 km) away.

howitzer–a cannon that shoots explosive shells long distances
cruise missile–a guided missile launched from a ship or aircraft that delivers an explosive warhead

M777 howitzer

VEHICLES

Aircraft

The United States had more money and better technology than the insurgents. The F-117 Nighthawk **stealth** fighters had advanced attack systems. These planes helped U.S. forces fly many successful missions. None of these planes were lost in combat.

stealth– having the ability to move without being seen by radar

F-117 Nighthawk

The A-10 Thunderbolt was a key
weapon at the beginning of the war.
It destroyed all of Saddam Hussein's
tanks. The A-10 Thunderbolt could fly
low and help troops on the ground.

A-10 Thunderbolt

Fact

The U.S. B-2 Spirit bomber
planes carried up to 40,000
pounds (18,000 kg) of weapons.

Tanks and Assault Vehicles

The United States had advanced tanks and **assault vehicles**. Most of these vehicles had thick armor. Armored vehicles safely moved troops.

assault vehicle—a combat vehicle, protected by strong armor and often armed with weapons

Fact

The U.S. M2 Bradley fighting vehicle had very thick armor. It protected soldiers from bullets and explosives.

In the beginning of the war, Iraqi forces used older tanks from China and the former Soviet Union. Insurgents sometimes used buses and trucks as combat vehicles.

T-72

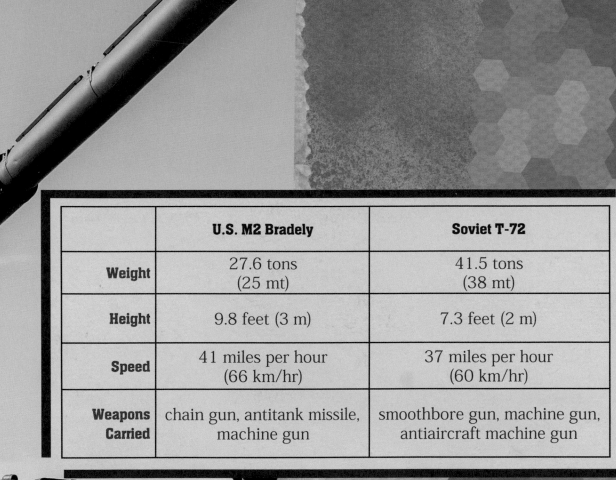

	U.S. M2 Bradely	Soviet T-72
Weight	27.6 tons (25 mt)	41.5 tons (38 mt)
Height	9.8 feet (3 m)	7.3 feet (2 m)
Speed	41 miles per hour (66 km/hr)	37 miles per hour (60 km/hr)
Weapons Carried	chain gun, antitank missile, machine gun	smoothbore gun, machine gun, antiaircraft machine gun

NEW TECHNOLOGIES

MQ-1 Predator

unmanned aerial vehicle–aircraft piloted by remote control

Unmanned Aerial Vehicles

Unmanned aerial vehicles (UAVs) were not new during the Iraq War. But they were lighter and better than before. The United States used UAVs to make attacks and to spy.

Fact

The U.S. military still uses many kinds of UAVs. The most famous is the MQ-1 Predator.

Locator Devices

U.S. troops used advanced technology to track enemies and keep from getting lost. **Global Positioning Systems** (GPS) guided soldiers on roads. **Thermal imaging** devices helped U.S. soldiers see enemies who were far away.

Fact

GPS technology greatly improved during the Iraq War. Soldiers using GPS could find their location with an accuracy of 10 feet (3 m).

Global Positioning System—a computer that receives signals from satellites
thermal imaging—using the heat given off by an object to create an image of it or locate it

Global Positioning System

GLOSSARY

ally (AL-eye)—a person or country that helps and supports another

assault vehicle (uh-SAWLT VEE-uh-kuhl)—a combat vehicle, protected by strong armor and often armed with weapons

combat (KOM-bat)—fighting between people or armies

cruise missile (KROOZ MISS-uhl)—a guided missile launched from a ship or aircraft that delivers an explosive warhead

Global Positioning System (GLOH-buhl puh-ZI-shuh-ning SISS-tuhm)—a computer that receives signals from satellites

howitzer (HOU-uht-sur)—a cannon that shoots explosive shells long distances

insurgent (in-SUR-juhnt)—a person who rebels and fights against his or her country's ruling government and those supporting it

range (RAYNJ)—the longest distance at which a weapon can still hit its target

stealth (STELTH)—having the ability to move without being seen by radar

thermal imaging (THUR-muhl IM-ij-ing)—using the heat given off by an object to create an image of it or locate it

unmanned aerial vehicle (UHN-mand AYR-ee-uhl VEE-uh-kuhl)—aircraft piloted by remote control

warfare (WAR-fayr)—the fighting of wars

weapon of mass destruction (WEP-uhn UHV MASS di-STRUHK-shuhn)—nuclear, radiological, biological, chemical, or another weapon that can kill or harm a large number of people

READ MORE

Brown, Don. *America is Under Attack.* Actual Times. New York: Roaring Book Press, 2011.

Samuels, Charlie. *Timeline of the War on Terror.* Americans at War. New York: Gareth Stevens Pub., 2012.

Shank, Carol. *U.S. Military Assault Vehicles.* U.S. Military Technology. North Mankato, Minn.: Capstone Pub., 2013.

INTERNET SITES

FactHound offers a safe, fun way to find Internet sites related to this book. All of the sites on FactHound have been researched by our staff

Here's all you do:

Visit *www.facthound.com*

Type in this code: 9781491440810

Check out projects, games and lots more at
www.capstonekids.com

INDEX